Kay
Woelfer

THE
RAINSTICK
PACK

SACRED EARTH

THE
RAINSTICK
PACK

*Explore the Mysteries
and Traditions of Native
Chilean Culture*

NICK CAISTOR

UNIVERSE

First published in the United States of America by
Universe Publishing
A Division of Rizzoli International Publications, Inc.
300 Park Avenue South
New York, NY 10010

ISBN 0-7893-0092-3

Library of Congress Catalog
Card number: 97-60898

The original paintings that appear in this book are
the work of Chilean artist Rocio Reyes-Cortez.
Born in 1971, she was educated in London and has
exhibited in England and Chile. Her paintings
express traditional concepts of Chilean spirituality
in a modern western context.

This book was conceived, designed and produced by
THE IVY PRESS LIMITED
2/3 St Andrews Place
Lewes, East Sussex
BN7 1UP

Art director: *Peter Bridgewater*
Designer: *Glyn Bridgewater*
Managing Editor: *Anne Townley*
Editor: *Tim Locke*
Picture research: *Vanessa Fletcher*
Studio photography: *Guy Ryecart*

Printed and bound in China

CONTENTS

INTRODUCTION

Raise the rainstick and tilt it gently: you hear the sound of tiny pebbles rushing over the thorns that have been pounded into the hollow cactus stem. You hear, too, the rains that are eagerly awaited in the Andean hillsides of the north of Chile, close to the high Atacama desert, one of the most arid regions on earth. On the rare occasions that it does rain there, the entire landscape comes to life with a bright, unsuspected green. The cacti burst into flower, and birds and insects magically appear from one moment to the next.

Our belief is that rainsticks, which have been made by native Chilean craftsmen, have long been used by the indigenous peoples of this part of South America not only to honor the cactus but also to call upon the gods to send the rains, while leaders of a group chant rhythmically. To ears accustomed to the machine cacophony of the late twentieth century, the rainstick has a mystic quality that evokes Chile's ethnic roots. Additionally, it soothes and lulls babies to sleep, it aids meditation, and it produces extraordinary effects as a percussion instrument in both Western and ethnic music.

In the pages that follow, we use the rainstick as the starting point of a journey to explore the world of the people, who have lived in Chile for thousands of years. We shall discover how they and their beliefs have evolved over the centuries. We shall see how they fought against conquest by Spaniards and other Europeans in order to keep alive

Meticulously crafted by hand, the rainstick re-creates the soothing, magical sound of pattering rain.

their sense of identity and system of values that may seem a mystery to outsiders. And we shall look at the crafts that they continue to make with great expertise and at their ceremonies and legends.

The native tribes have gradually adapted to their harsh landscapes. They have learned to use whatever nature has to offer, whether for farming the land or building their communities – the cactus wood you are holding was gathered from the cactus "forests" by local families after the natural death of these plants. The native peoples have celebrated the life-giving properties of rain in many ceremonies. Together with the sun, the moon, and the gods of the volcanoes that rise in the Andes mountain chain along the length of Chile, they have worshiped the blessings of the rain.

Some lifestyles – such as those of the original peoples of Easter Island and Tierra del Fuego – have vanished forever. Yet other groups, such as the Mapuche of central Chile, retain their traditional ways despite pressures to cede to outside influence. These indigenous peoples of Chile have much to teach us. Through the thousands of years that they have spent on one land, they have forged a unique view of the world around them. As you listen to the pebbles cascading through the rainstick, perhaps you can conjure up even more from their country: the sands of the north, the Pacific Ocean buffeting the long Chilean coastline, the wind sighing in the araucaria pines of the south. Perhaps, too, you will hear their voices, echoing softly from a distant land.

THE RAINSTICK STORY

THE RAINSTICK is a gift from South America to the rest of the world. Simple yet endlessly fascinating, it is truly a "people's artifact" made from the local materials at hand and designed to call up the fundamental spirit of the rain.

A horseman at an Easter Fiesta: such festvities and ceremonies are undergoing a revival in Chile today.

Rainsticks are found as far north as Mexico and in Chile, Ecuador, and Brazil. As far as we know, the history of the rainstick is, appropriately, a people's history: that is, a history that is undocumented in literature. Yet it is not difficult to imagine how it developed. The appeal of the rainstick is universal: evoking rain, copying the sound it makes pattering onto leaves – not the raw power of a storm, but a gentle, revitalizing shower – and finally bringing fertility to all enterprises. While it is easy to imagine an ornate ceremonial rainstick used by a high priest to call on a rain god, such as the Incan Illrapa, it fits much better into a humbler, more domestic picture: an anxious farmer tilting his home-made rainstick as he prays for rain to feed his maize crop.

The rainstick is equally at home in lighthearted musical celebrations. In the West, this aspect has great appeal, and musical groups use rainsticks to provide an evocative background sound.

HOLLOW CACTUS STEM   CACTUS THORNS   PEBBLES

. The rainstick's simplicity is evident in the cross-section above. Rainsticks can be made in all sizes, depending on the cactus available, from the small one in this pack to full size sticks as tall as a person.

HOW THE RAINSTICK IS MADE

Rainsticks can be made from bamboo, but in Chile they are made from the dead wood of the cactus *Eulychnia acida* or *Echinopsis chiloensis* that grow in the deserts of the north. First the wood is gathered, along with the cactus thorns. The thorns are then

Cactus, the source material for the Chilean rainstick.

pounded through the hollow tube of the cactus wood. Once one end of the rainstick has been sealed with a wooden cap, tiny pebbles are poured into the hollow stick before the other end is similarly sealed, and the rainstick is ready for use.

Of all the South American countries, Chile has been the most active in bringing the rainstick to the West. Most of these rainsticks are made in the traditional way by Chilean people.

9

THE RAIN STICK

Upend the rain stick and what happens next
Is a music that you never would have known
To listen for. In a cactus stalk

Downpour, sluice-rush, spillage and backwash
Come flowing through. You stand there like a pipe
Being played by water, you shake it again lightly

And diminuendo runs through all its scales
Like a gutter stopping trickling. And now here comes
A sprinkle of drops out of the freshened leaves,

Then subtle little wets off grass and daisies;
Then glitter-drizzle, almost-breaths of air.
Upend the stick again. What happens next

Is undiminished for having happened once,
Twice, ten, a thousand times before.
Who cares if all the music that transpires

Is the fall of grit or dry seeds through a cactus?
You are like a rich man entering heaven
Through the ear of a raindrop. Listen now again.

SEAMUS HEANEY

THE PEOPLES
OF CHILE

MANY INHABITANTS of the fertile highlands of north, where terraced fields still dominate much of the landscape, can claim to be descendants of the first peoples of Chile. The population gradually crept southward; the Mapuche, Picunche, and Huilliche peoples, known collectively as Araucanians, settled in central and southern Chile. In the bleak wilds of the far south, the Fuegians were the last natives to keep free of Western influence, living in leaderless communities dependent on mutual trust.

Following a century of Inca rule, the arrival of the Spaniards in the sixteenth century signaled a bloody period of conquest and counterattack. The legacy of nearly two and a half centuries of colonial rule includes the cities the Spanish conquerors founded and the Spanish language imposed on the people they vanquished.

Early European travelers looked down upon the natives and believed them to be savages or even giants. Missionaries sought to enlighten them, and in a farcical episode a Captain Robert Fitzroy attempted to give three natives an English education. Peruvians took most of the inhabitants of Easter Island as slaves, effectively ending a centuries-old civilization whose vanished culture will forever remain an enigma. Yet the eccentric Frenchman Orillie-Antoine endeared himself sufficiently to the Mapuche that they allowed him to impose his own monarchy.

Even today native tribes continue to have a mistrust of outsiders, as well as a superstitious fear of the north, from where their invaders originally came and where evil is said to reside.

CHILE'S FIRST PEOPLES

IN SIZE, APPEARANCE, and blood types, peoples of the Americas and of Asia share strikingly common characteristics. The Asians are believed to have been the first to have crossed to the American continent some time between 40,000 and 25,000 years ago. At that time the huge buildup of ice during the Ice Age caused sea levels to be lower, so there was a land bridge between the two continents. This enabled the first wandering tribes to explore a new world.

Archeological evidence points to a gradual spread of population southward through the American continent over the next 20,000 years. By that reckoning, Chile and Argentina would have been the last countries in South America to have been populated, probably around 15000 B.C. The earliest traces of prehistoric man discovered at the southernmost tip of the continent are thought to date from 9000 B.C.

These first peoples spread down southward through the foothills of the Andes mountains. The vast Atacama desert, which includes some of the most inhospitable land in the world, deterred these groups from populating any part of Chile other than the mountain valleys and the seashores.

Our understanding of these inhabitants is scant, but ancient sites give some clues about their lifestyles. At Tagua Tagua, in the north of Chile, evidence has come to light that native peoples hunted mammoth and used fire to make pots. Another site, preserved under a layer of peat at Monteverde, probably dates from about 12000 B.C. Here archeologists found five skeletons of mastodons, a relative of the mammoth, which had been killed for meat, as well as freshwater shellfish. They also discovered evidence that these first Chileans had eaten seeds and berries, and used implements made of bone, wood, and stone.

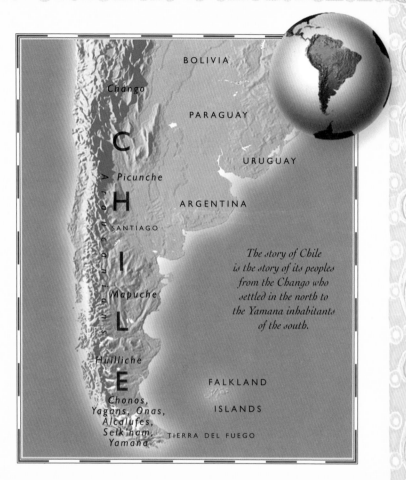

BOLIVIA

Chango

PARAGUAY

C

URUGUAY

H

Picunche

ARGENTINA

I

SANTIAGO

The story of Chile
is the story of its peoples
from the Chango who
settled in the north to
the Yamana inhabitants
of the south.

L

Mapuche

Huilliche

FALKLAND

E

Chonos,
Yagans, Onas,
Alcalufes,
Selk'nam,
Yamana

ISLANDS

TIERRA DEL FUEGO

THE CHANGO OF THE NORTH

Some early Chileans lived in the Atacama and the northern
Andes; they were in contact with the civilizations that developed
in the more fertile central Andes highlands in Bolivia and Peru.
Gradually these people began to cultivate the land, building
terraces and using irrigation canals to spread water through their
fields. These people – generally known as the Chango – constructed walled fortifications and had weapons and leather armor.

13

The present-day inhabitants of the Lasana Valley of the Atacama desert still cultivate their land in the system of terraces developed by their Chango forebears.

About two to three thousand years ago, these indigenous tribes began to domesticate animals both for their milk and for their meat. They raised llamas and apparently regarded guinea pigs as a special delicacy. They used llama wool for making textiles, dyed with very bright colors. Even today, some of the world's finest rugs and ponchos are still being produced in this region.

They also began to grow crops, including maize, quinoa, and the humble potato, as described many years later by Charles Darwin, who visited Chile during his historic round-the-world voyage on HMS *Beagle*.

An alpaca, a domesticated relative of the llama.

THE ARAUCANIAN TRIBES

Known generically as Araucanians, the people of the comparative-ly fertile lands of central and southern Chile formed three distinct groups. To the north lived the Picunche, in the center were the Mapuche, and to the south of them was the territory of the

Huilliche. In comparison with the northerners, the Araucanians found their land more fertile and easier to adapt to.

Similarities in their dwellings, pottery, and other remains suggest that they may have been greatly influenced by the nomads who roved the pampas areas of Argentina. The Araucanians started agriculture some five or six thousand years ago, growing maize and other crops, keeping llama herds – which provided meat, milk, and wool – as well as gathering wild fruit such as hazelnuts and the Chilean strawberry, which they use even today for its medicinal properties.

Because of the favorable terrain, these tribes lived in larger groups, typically of several hundred people. They built adobes, or mud-brick houses, the size of which was restricted by the frequent earthquakes that still strike Chile today. Archeologists have unearthed bones that were adapted into flutes; these and other bones are believed to have been those of enemies, indicating that the three groups fought each other regularly.

Chile's long coastline ensures that fishing is a way of life, with the inhabitants of the coastal region inheriting a long canoe-making tradition.

*Some of the last survivors of a traditional way of life – a Yagan
family captured on film outside their hut in the late nineteenth century.*

The peoples of the central Chilean coast were expert canoe-
makers, crafting their vessels from wood and seal hides.
Similarities in the canoes, huts, and implements made by Chileans
and Polynesians have prompted some archeologists to speculate
that the first peoples of the South American continent arrived
from Polynesia, far away in the south Pacific Ocean.

For many years, too, there was a far-fetched theory in circu-
lation based on a legend that Chinese statues had been found in
southern Chile. Some writers suggested that the Chilean indigenous people were in fact part of the ancient civilizations of the
Orient – had not Columbus originally thought he had discovered
the lands of the Great Khan?

HUNTERS OF THE FAR SOUTH

On the cold coasts and islands of the west and in the archipelago
of Tierra del Fuego, the indigenous groups of Chonos, Yagans,
Onas, Selk'nam, Yamana, and Alcalufes were even more isolated
than the other Chileans, partly by geography, partly by the nature

of their social organization. They apparently lived in self-contained family groups of about 20 or 30 people, hunting and scavenging, making their shelters from wood, whale bones, and seal hides. Their isolation meant that effectively they were, more than any other group, the direct descendants of the first people to settle in Chile many thousands of years earlier. Left untouched by the Spanish conquest, they remained completely outside the influence of the rest of the world until the last hundred years.

THE BEGINNINGS OF VILLAGE CULTURE

About 2,500 years ago, the first villages appeared. The earliest traces of pottery yet found date from around 1000 B.C. Except for the evidence of fighting between the different groups, little has come down to us of the structure of their societies, and we have sketchy knowledge of their beliefs and gods. Some graves have shown that dogs were buried with their masters to accompany them in the next world, a practice still carried out in the mountainous regions of northern Chile and Argentina.

The indigenous tribes in Chile were too isolated and too few in number to develop any strong, centrally controlled society such as those found in Mexico or Peru. Until the arrival of the Spaniards, their means of transportation were very limited, since they had neither horses nor the use of the wheel. It was only in the far north and in the highlands that they became part of larger empires. Here, the Aymara from Peru and the Quechua people based in Tiahuanaco in Bolivia exerted their control. It was they who brought to Chile the ceremonial worship of Viracocha – the bearded white-skinned god who created the other gods as well as all animals and men. Remains have also shown that these northern groups worshiped Inti, the god of the sun, from whom all the Incan emperors were thought to have descended.

Despite only a brief stay, the Incas left many marks of their occupation on the landscape, including these rock paintings in the Atacama desert.

INCAS AND SPANIARDS

Not until the fifteenth century did the Incas directly take control in Chile. They established their system of roads for messengers, exacted tribute, and even sent settlers to colonize parts of the north of the country. The Incas' well-developed organization brought the remote tribes under some degree of rule from Cuzco, the imperial capital. Yet soon the Inca empire had to meet the formidable challenge of the Spanish invaders, and this led to the collapse of their influence in Chile.

A beaten gold mask of the Incan sun god Inti. Gold was seen as "the sweat of the sun".

The lives of most native Chileans were shaken in the mid-sixteenth century by the arrival of a force from outside: the Spanish conquerors. At the time when the Spaniards sought to expand their conquests from Mexico and Central America down the moun-

18

tain chain of the Andes, there were perhaps about ten million indigenous inhabitants in the region. Of these, it has been calculated that there were about a million living in Chile. Many were soon killed; those who survived found that their old way of life – with all its attendant beliefs – was to be swept away forever.

THE MUMMY OF EL PLOMO MOUNTAIN

One of the most extraordinary finds from the days of the Incas is the preserved corpse of a boy aged nine or ten. It was found in 1954 by a shoemaker and amateur archeologist on El Plomo mountain close to the capital Santiago. In a circle of stones near the summit, he stumbled upon this corpse, perfectly preserved by the everlasting snows, hunched up under a cloak. The boy was wearing a headdress of black and white condor feathers, and next to his body were small statues of a llama, a deer, and an Indian woman. Although he had not been mummified in the technical sense, he became dubbed the Mummy of El Plomo mountain.

The Natural History Museum in Santiago pronounced it to be 450 years old, dating from the Inca period. What most amazed the experts was the quiet calm of the boy's face, painted red and with four broad yellow stripes running down from the corners of his eyes to his mouth. According to the museum, the boy must have been brought hundreds of miles to the mountain as a sacrifice to the god of the sun. He had been drugged or given alcohol, then left for the cold to claim his life. "He looked just as if he would

The lama, the first animal to reappear after the Great Flood, is honored all over South America.

wake up if we touched his shoulder," explained the shoemaker. The "mummy" is the only known example of human sacrifice in Chile.

A CLASH OF CULTURES

Ferdinand Magellan (1480–1521) encountered the "giants" of Tierra del Fuego on his last voyage.

To the first European explorers, who ventured to the American continent from the late fifteenth century onward, the indigenous people were a source of intrigue and bafflement. The accounts of sailors, who were the earliest voyagers to what became known as Patagonia at the tip of mainland Argentina and Chile, show that they believed the natives they had encountered were monsters with magical – and mostly evil – characteristics.

One of the pioneers was Antonio Pigafetta, a survivor of the first round-the-world voyage (1519–22) by the Portuguese navigator Magellan. Pigafetta wrote the first account of a meeting with the indigenous groups of Tierra del Fuego. From the outset he regarded them as not human:

"One day, without anyone expecting it, we saw a giant, who was on the shore of the sea, quite naked, and was dancing and leaping, and singing, and while singing he put the sand and dust on his head. Our captain sent one of his men toward him, who he charged to sing and leap like the other to reassure him, and show him friendship. Immediately the sailor led this giant to a little island where the captain was waiting for him; and when he was before us he began to be astonished, and to be afraid, and he raised one finger on high, thinking that we came from heaven. He was so tall that the tallest of us only came up to his waist."

Magellan decided to take two of these Patagonians to the court of Charles V, the Holy Roman Emperor. On board ship, Pigafetta also saw them as very strange creatures: "These two giants that we had in the ship ate a large basketful of biscuits, and rats without skinning them, and they drank half a bucket of water at each time." The courts of Europe were unable to judge just how human these strange people were: both "giants" died of disease while Magellan was crossing the Pacific Ocean.

Nevertheless, the tale of these enormous folk at the far ends of the earth did enter the European consciousness. Pigafetta's giants are even thought to have been the inspiration for Shakespeare's monstrous beings in his magical play *The Tempest*.

A CHANGELESS PEOPLE

Even when much of the rest of the continent was explored, the coasts of the far south still kept their secrets. When Charles Darwin visited them more than three hundred years after Pigafetta, he still saw the inhabitants as "savages", whose way of life only inspired pity and a reflection on "civilized" man:

"December 17th, 1832... When we came within hail, one of the four natives who were present advanced to receive us, and began to shout most vehemently, wishing to direct us where to land. When we were on shore the party looked

A man of the Tekeenica tribe. Such peoples were an anthropological curiosity to early explorers.

rather alarmed, but continued talking and making gestures with great rapidity. It was without exception the most curious and interesting spectacle I ever beheld: I could not have believed how wide was the difference between savage and civilized man; it is greater than that between a wild and domesticated animal, inasmuch as in man there is a greater power of improvement."

This attitude of complete superiority lasted well into the present century, and was not confined to Europeans. The Chilean author Agustin Edwards wrote of the Alcalufes of Tierra del Fuego in *Peoples of Old* (1924): "They are human amphibians who are still living in a state of complete degradation and savagery, and have up to the present resisted all attempts to educate and civilize them."

Early encounters between the native peoples of Chile and early explorers were as bewildering for one as for the other.

In Praise of
THE SIMPLE PEOPLE
OF THESE LANDS

THE CLEAREST appreciation of the worth of these southern
tribes is found in the writings of a Spanish soldier who came to
conquer them. In the sixteenth century Alonso de Ercilla was
part of the first expeditions against the Araucanians of southern
Chile. After he had retired from fighting, he wrote *La Araucana*
– the epic of Araucania – one of the most extraordinary long
poems ever written in Latin America. Ercilla had no doubt as to
the value of the indigenous way of life, or who was to blame for
its ultimate destruction:

> *The sincere goodness and affection*
> *of the simple people of these lands*
> *forced me to realize that greed*
> *had not yet gained a foothold on those heights*
> *nor had wrongdoing, theft, or injustice*
> *– the staple fare of any war –*
> *found here the slightest*
> *echo or undermined their natural law.*
>
> *We it was who set out to destroy*
> *all we came upon in our path*
> *forcing a way with our usual arrogance*
> *and opening the door wide to all these ills;*
> *so their ancient laws became corrupted,*
> *ruined by a stream of insults*
> *and soon greed planted its banner*
> *even more firmly than elsewhere.*

CANTO XXXII

THE LAND OF FIRE

SCATTERED OFF the southern tip of the American continent, the archipelago of Tierra del Fuego – the "land of fire" – was probably the last area in Chile to be inhabited during the gradual spread of people farther and farther southward. Because of the region's remoteness and harsh climate, the indigenous groups survived into modern times as those Chileans least affected by Western civilization.

For thousands of years, the three main groups of Fuegians – the Yamana, the Selk'nam, and the Alcalufes – led a semi-nomadic existence. They hunted animals such as deer and seals on land, or lived off the supplies of fish

The inhospitable terrain of Tierra del Fuego protected its population from outside influence.

and shellfish that were found in abundance on the seashores. The Fuegians adapted to survive the near-constant strong westerly winds and the deep snows of winter, wearing thick animal skins and inhabiting wooden huts covered with hides or leaves.

Contact with Europeans and other Chileans was infrequent. Sailors struggling around Cape Horn were occasionally forced to shelter among them. Some attempts at colonization were made, but soon abandoned because of the appalling climate and lack of food. Although Tierra del Fuego was nominally part of Chile, few state representatives ever made the journey this far south.

THE NEW WHITE SETTLERS

It was only at the end of the nineteenth century that the outside world began to take a sustained interest in this remote area. The first missionaries came, with their desire to save the souls of these "unenlightened people." Settlers, mostly sheep ranchers and sawmill owners, were more concerned to clear the "Indians" off land that they claimed as their own. Photographs from the turn of the twentieth century show that they even hired gunmen to go on shooting parties and rid the country of them. One Belgian sea captain, Albert Lecointe, wrote at this time: "The Indians have received such dreadful treatment from the white man that they are full of hatred and are driven to committing criminal acts. The white people then punish them for this, and so these tribes are slowly but surely being exterminated."

Those Fuegians who did not die from this brutality often fell victim to the diseases caught from the "white man" in the missionary schools or trading posts that the newcomers set up. What had happened more than four centuries earlier in many other parts of Latin America and the Caribbean, took place in the far south just two or three generations ago.

The Fuegians used the building materials that were readily at hand — seal hides or leaves.

ANTHROPOLOGY WITH RESPECT

One extraordinary witness to the way the communities were being driven to extinction was the Austrian anthropologist Martin Gusinde. He spent much of the period from 1918 to 1924 among them, and left an invaluable record in both words and photographs of their vanishing way of life.

Gusinde showed the indigenous people a respect rare among Europeans coming into contact with them. He was deeply impressed by the harmonious way they had adapted to the difficult natural conditions they lived in and by the social organization that ensured their survival. The Alcalufe, Selk'nam, and Yamanas rewarded his respect by giving him insights into their way of life and their jealously guarded secrets probably never seen by an outsider before, and certainly not since. Such was the reticence of the groups that, for example, none of them named their Supreme Being directly, but instead used formulas such as "the old man in the sky" and "the very ancient one."

They had no leaders, nor any single figure of authority. Instead, the whole community exerted its pressure on the individual, placing reliance on a concept of good and evil provided by their religious beliefs, which were also passed on collectively.

THE INITIATION OF YOUNG ADULTS

Gusinde had the great privilege to be allowed to participate in the entire initiation ceremony that young Yamana boys and girls have to go through before they are accepted as "good and worthwhile" members of the adult community.

The process of initiating the new adults took several weeks. It began when the Yamana group succeeded in harpooning a whale. This guaranteed them enough food to enable the Yamana community to leave its usual daily search for sustenance, and to dedicate themselves to the rigorous ceremony, which lasted several weeks. It began with the construction of a ceremonial hut, a long wooden structure like an upturned boat, covered with leaves, with two low openings at each end. Once this had been built, and the entrances painted with black, white, and red stripes to keep off the evil spirits, the group chose someone to lead the young people through their initiation. This was apparently the only time that the Yamana ever had a leader, and it was strictly for this ceremonial purpose only. They also chose an "inspector," who would guarantee that each step of the ceremony was being properly carried out. Another was made the "scarecrow": during the ceremony, he was painted white all over, with red stripes running up from the palms of his hands. His job was to scare away small children and others who should not know the secrets of the initiation.

Body painting – part of ceremonial ritual – served to enhance the formidable appearance of the "scarecrow."

FEATS OF ENDURANCE

The boys and girls chosen for the ceremony, normally around the age of puberty, were then seized from their parents' homes and taken to the ceremonial hut. Each boy was placed between a man and a woman, each girl between two women. These adults were the "godparents" of the initiates, giving them encouragement and making sure they understood all the stages of the ritual.

This began with teaching the youngsters that they must be able to control their bodies and their appetites. The candidates were made to squat down, with their arms folded across their chest, and their heads resting on their arms. They were to stay in this squatting position all the time they were in the communal hut, and to sleep in the same way too. To test their self-control, their godparents would put grubs in their hair or on their backs, to make sure they would not move.

Fuegian initiation rites include ceremonial face painting for both boys and girls.

Control of their bodies in this way was taken as a sign that they were true masters of their minds and desires as well. The candidates were also made to go without much food for the whole of the initiation, something Gusinde found particularly grueling. In his journal, he complains that "each day all we were given to eat was one oyster and a piece of meat about as big as a frankfurter."

The next stage of the ritual was to teach them the traditional tasks assigned to the men and women of the community. After snatching what sleep they could in their squatting position, they were awakened before dawn by a sharp blow on the back from one of their godparents. Thus stirred into action for a new day, the candidates would paint their faces with white lines radiating down from their eyes. When they were ready, the boys and girls were then led off in different directions.

The boys were taken to the woods to chop wood and haul it to the camp. They were taught how to harpoon fish and use a bow and arrow. They were made to stand for hours in the freezing water, and to paddle canoes all day. The girls were taught to make baskets, to cure skins and hides, and to search the seashore for crabs, sea urchins, and oysters.

This course of instruction lasted for most of the day, over a period of weeks until the adults were satisfied that their charges had properly learned their tasks. Every day in the late afternoon, all of the candidates were taken back to the main hut. They ate their meager meal, then listened while the chosen leader imparted the moral lessons they also needed to learn to be full and useful members of their community.

CODES OF CONDUCT

These lessons included a series of "commandments" on how to behave – inspired by the fear and respect the Yamanas had for their god, but translated into very concrete terms, as shown by their recommendations on why someone should not steal. Gusinde recorded the leader instructing the group of initiates:

"You should never steal anything from anybody, particularly from anyone who is sick or handicapped. If you need something, ask your neighbor for it. But you have no right to take anything. This would soon be noticed, and everyone would understand that you have stolen it. And if you should find something by chance, don't say to yourself 'this belongs to me,' because its real owner will soon appear. If he sees the lost object in your hands, he will point it out to others and tell them: 'that man is a thief.' Then it could well be that the owner of the object brings his friends to destroy all your possessions, and to take a hammer to your canoe, so that you end up with nothing because you stole. No Yamana can tolerate a thief."

DANCING, STORY-TELLING, AND FEASTING

As well as this moral instruction, the afternoons in the ceremonial hut saw the whole community dancing, or the old people telling the tribe's legends, or their personal experiences of meeting spirits. Often the story-telling was accompanied by a low, monotonous chanting or keening, which went on all night. So the whole community participated in the initiation process, using it as a way of reaffirming their own beliefs and bringing them together once more as a group.

The initiation ceremony could last more than a month. By the end of it, the young candidates were exhausted and hungry. But they had absorbed the community's religious and moral beliefs, and were ready to play their full part in its future. The community itself had also strengthened its links. The adults had also been able to judge the new generation and, thanks to all the tests they had set them, could reassure themselves that they could fit in to the harsh world facing them.

To end the ceremony, the whole group held a great feast when all the remaining food was eaten up before everyone resumed their normal life. As a gift at the close of the ceremony, the new adults were given a hollow bird's bone to use as a straw to drink water through – a symbol of all they had learned during the initiation process – and a scraper to scratch with. From then on, these would be worn on a thong around the neck.

*Using the protection of thick animal skins the
Fuegians adapted to survive the region's harsh climate.*

THE LAST DAYS OF THE FUEGIANS

Gusinde left Tierra del Fuego in 1924. He himself was horrified at the way the numbers of Fuegians were diminishing. He calculated that the indigenous people remaining on Tierra del Fuego and the surrounding islands numbered only 600. He proposed that these should be gathered together in reservations on some of the larger islands. Any economic exploitation of the islands would then be forbidden, as would the settlement by any "white people." He concluded bitterly: "These proposals, which did not involve any economic or administrative burden for the Chilean state, would to my mind have permitted the survival of the last Fuegians. But I met with not the slightest comprehension of my ideas, and so the last groups of indigenous peoples on Tierra del Fuego – so important for our understanding of the history of mankind's culture – have been disappearing before our very eyes." Today only a handful of the Alcalufe survive – the last remnants on Tierra del Fuego of a civilization that stretches back over 10,000 years.

THE MYSTERIES
OF EASTER ISLAND

THE TRIANGULAR volcanic outcrop known as Easter Island lies almost 2,400 miles (3,800 kilometers) west of mainland Chile. Despite its modest size – only about 97 square miles (250 square kilometers) – it has posed a gigantic enigma for explorers and scientists for centuries.

It takes the name Easter Island because of its discovery during Holy Week in 1722 by the Dutch navigator Jacobo Roggeveen (1659–1729). He was amazed to find that such a lonely island had a thriving indigenous population. Roggeveen noted that there seemed to be two different groups, one far lighter-skinned than the other, and saw them worshiping huge stone statues and bowing to the sun at dawn. The islanders gave him a hostile reception, and unfortunately their subsequent history was ultimately as tragic as that of many other ethnic peoples.

THE END OF A CIVILIZATION

Visited occasionally by explorers – among them Captain Cook – the population of several thousand islanders remained stable until the middle of the nineteenth century, when a fleet from Peru took most of them into captivity. Christian missionaries reported this action, which provoked such an international outcry that the Peruvians finally agreed to return the surviving islanders. But by the time they got back, no more than 15 prisoners were still alive. Worse still, the diseases, especially smallpox, that these people had picked up while in forced labor in Peru caused such havoc among

A female native of Easter Island, painted during Captain Cook's voyage.

When Captain James Cook
(1728–79) traveled to the South Pacific
in the 1770s the population of
Easter Island was still relatively intact.

the remaining 5,000 inhabitants still on Easter Island that 80 percent of them were wiped out. Following their unhappy demise, all knowledge of the ancient civilization on the island rapidly dwindled to nothing.

This maltreatment continued after the island formally became part of Chilean national territory in 1888. The surviving population was forced to live in villages, while the green grasslands of the island were given over to an English ranching company for the purpose of raising flocks of sheep, cattle, and horses. The islanders' neglect continued into the twentieth century. In 1934 the anthropologist Alfred Metraux commented:

"There is so much misery on Easter Island that it would be wrong to speak of any transition from a primitive state to civilization. Due to neglect by the Chileans, or even worse, due to the harmful influence of the people sent out there, the island has not so much fallen into decay as simply rotted away, in the midst of hopeless misery."

Today the island's situation has improved, thanks to the interests of scientists and tourists: one-third of it is protected as a national park, and the inhabitants' way of life is respected.

CLUES TO THE RIDDLE

International scientists have visited Easter Island for many reasons. A particular source of intrigue is the question of how such a tiny, isolated island – as far from Chile as from the nearest Polynesian islands – came to be inhabited at all. The stone dwellings of the first inhabitants, some of them shaped like elongated boats, were similar to those found in Polynesia, but for many years experts doubted that primitive people could have had sufficient navigational skills to find what is virtually a speck in the ocean, and to keep contact with any colony living there.

THE KON-TIKI EXPEDITION

In 1947 the Norwegian anthropologist Thor Heyerdahl made his famous voyage on the raft Kon-Tiki. His purpose was to prove that early peoples could have sailed between South America and the Pacific islands. Using only tools available to early men, Heyerdahl constructed a balsawood raft and sailed successfully across the Pacific, from Peru to the islands of Tuamotu.

Heyerdahl also argued that the two groups on the island – as seen by Roggeveen in 1722 – were what he called the LongEars (whose earlobes were lengthened by heavy earrings) and the ShortEars. According to him, the short-eared group rose up against

their long-eared masters, and massacred nearly all of them sometime in the late seventeenth century.

Petroglyphs – rock pictures – are one of the mysteries of Easter Island.

What is the significance of the moais of Easter Island? Many anthropologists and explorers have speculated upon their meaning and purpose, but with no definite conclusion.

More recent scientists have dismissed this theory as too fanciful, and concluded that the island was populated from farther west in the Pacific, rather than from the South American mainland, probably about a thousand years ago.

Once he had landed on Easter Island, Heyerdahl also tried to resolve one of the most puzzling problems there. This concerns the hundreds of huge statues scattered around the island. Known as "moais," these huge representations of the face and upper bodies of men or gods stand between 13 and 30 feet (4–9 meters) tall, and are carved from solid volcanic rock. Buried up to the waist, these stern-featured giants have become famous throughout the world. But how could the early people have transported them, and how could they have raised them vertically? Again, Heyerdahl used only materials available at that earlier time – levers, wooden rollers, and stones – to see if it were possible to erect them. He and his colleagues succeeded in moving them many miles and raising them without the aid of modern technology.

UNANSWERED QUESTIONS

But that did not solve the main mystery of the moais: their meaning, and for what purpose they were used. They clearly had some religious significance: but why, for example, were most of them facing toward the interior of the island, whereas only a few of them faced out to sea? Why had a whole group of the oldest ones been deliberately pushed down and disfigured?

Their significance lost – the moais represent a time when the gods were revered and worshiped.

No-one has yet come up with convincing answers to these questions, despite many fascinating discoveries. One of the most important of these was the quarry on the slopes of the Rano-Raruka volcano from which most of the statues were taken. But even this find created as many questions as it resolved. Still in the quarry were more than two hundred statues in various stages of preparation. Were these abandoned, perhaps because of the threat of an eruption? Others offer a simpler explanation: the families who ordered the sculptors to make the statues found they could not pay, so the artifacts were left unfinished.

Another Easter Island puzzle is that of the petroglyphs, or picture writings on the rocks throughout the island. These are carvings in the shape of birds, trees, and turtles. They even included depictions of monkeys, which have never existed on the island. Once again, the paintings seem to have had some religious meaning, but they have so far resisted any precise interpretation. An exception is the story of the "birdman of Orongo." Orongo was a center of island life in early times, and

Two birdmen of Orongo —
representations of a lost
ritual of village life.

the rocks on the beach nearby are covered with these carvings. One theory is that the recurring motif of a birdman holding an egg tells of a yearly ritual in which the young men of the village had to swim out to the islet of Motu-Kaokao, where migrating seabirds nested each spring. The first to return with an unbroken new egg was then chosen as the village leader for the year.

The islanders' script is also found on wooden tablets, one face of which is covered with many lines of tiny pictures, which are read alternately from right to left then left to right. Most of these rongo-rongo, as they are known, were destroyed in the nineteenth century by missionaries, who regarded them as being idolatrous; barely more than 20 have survived. Once again, their precise meaning remains a mystery. The most recent theory is that they are "creation songs," describing the creation of the world and its life, and were written down after the first contact with Europeans in the eighteenth century. Unfortunately, because of the disastrous consequences of that contact, the secret of the writing, as with that of the enigmatic statues, has probably been lost.

THE SPANISH INVASION

T HE SPANIARDS arrived in Chile in the second wave of their conquest of the Americas. Following Columbus's voyages of discovery at the end of the fifteenth century, they had already established themselves in the Caribbean, in Mexico, and in the north of the continent. In an audacious stroke, Francisco Pizarro took over the entire Inca empire in Peru by capturing the emperor Atahualpa and eventually killing him, although not before a ransom demand from the Spaniards had forced the Incas to collect enough gold and silver to fill a large room. Even by the standards of the conquest, this represented fabulous wealth, and it encouraged the Spaniards to make the Inca capital, Cuzco, one of the main centers of their own empire.

By 1535 the first expedition had set off from Peru to explore some of the wild terrain that makes up part of present-day Chile. Diego de Almagro left Cuzco with fewer than a hundred men. They explored the coastline down as far as the Maule River, more than 1,500 miles (2,400 kilometers) south. But in their travels they found no great riches or any developed cities like those that they had taken over in Peru. A year later Almagro returned to Cuzco; he had failed either to found any settlements or to conquer any of the natives.

COLONIZATION AND RESISTANCE

It was Pedro de Valdivia who really began the conquest and colonization of this new territory. Setting out from Cuzco with 150 men in 1541, he founded the settlement of Nueva Extremadura, now the Chilean capital Santiago. He went on to found Concepción, and farther south the town of Valdivia. These three settlements close to the coast became the country's major centers over the next three centuries.

The next year, however, saw the start of what was to become several centuries of resistance by the native Mapuche peoples, who rose up against the Spaniards in December 1553. In a skirmish, they killed three Spaniards, apparently the first time they had inflicted fatalities on their enemy. They now saw for themselves that the white men in their steel armor – which was far stronger than their own leather protection – were not immortal. The Mapuche also discovered that the Spaniards' horses – animals they had never before encountered – were separate beasts from their riders and also mortal in themselves. In their attempts to be rid of the Spaniards, the Mapuche were boosted by finding a leader in the figure of Lautaro. He confirmed to his companions that the Spaniards were essentially no different from them.

Their first great battle took place near the Spanish fort of Tucapel in January 1554, in which every Spanish defender perished. Valdivia himself met a dreadful fate, as related by a contemporary chronicle: "Valdivia was cruelly tortured. Although the Indians had the swords and poniards they had taken from their vanquished enemies, they preferred to use seashells, which they used as knives. With these they cut off his arms and, after having slightly roasted them, devoured them before his eyes."

Encouraged by this first victory, the Mapuche under Lautaro pushed further north. They destroyed the Spanish forts, and even overran the town of Concepción. But they made the mistake of advancing too far from their own territories and becoming isolated and vulnerable. In 1557, a Spanish force surrounded Lautaro and his Mapuche warriors and killed nearly all of them. The unrest over the next two hundred years followed a common pattern: resistance by the Mapuche, who succeeded in forcing the Spaniards back to the north, followed by massive retribution when the natives became too bold.

SOUTHWARD EXPANSION

The Spanish commander, Don Garcia Hurtado de Mendoza, then set about rebuilding the Spanish forts and pushed on further south, almost as far as the island of Chiloé. The Spanish firearms proved more than a match for the Mapuche, who relied on strength of numbers, often charging in the thousands at the tiny number of Spaniards so that they could overwhelm them in hand-to-hand combat with clubs and spears.

In 1558, the second great Mapuche leader, Caupolican, was captured by the Spaniards. They avenged the cruel death of Valdivia by impaling Caupolican alive on a sharpened stake in front of his companions. The Spanish occupation of Chile, particularly to the south of the Bio-Bio River, was rarely peaceful for long. Even today indigenous groups celebrate their great leaders such as Lautaro and Caupolican, and their repeated victories over the Spanish soldiers who tried to destroy their way of life.

But the Spaniards kept returning and gradually imposed their ways on much of the territory. Chile was never as important a center for the Spaniards as either Mexico or Peru. The Spaniards spread gradually southward but never established themselves in comparable numbers in southern Argentina and Chile. A key factor hindering the development of the south was that all trade had to be sold to Spain, requiring goods to be taken north to the ports in Peru or the Caribbean.

FORCED LABOR

Most new Spanish settlers devoted themselves to agriculture. They raised cattle, grew grain, and planted the first vines, thus beginning Chile's status as a wine producer. Spanish farmers adopted the ecomienda system used throughout their conquered territories, in which natives of conquered lands effectively

Throughout its long history, and despite the many incursions into its territory, Chile has remained largely an agricultural region.

became slaves, who were then shared out between the commanders and officers according to rank.

Royal decrees from Spain demanded that Spaniards in the colonies should care for the spiritual and physical welfare of the Indians in their charge, by converting them to Christianity and promoting their health and development. Often these decrees were ignored, and the native laborers sparked off new revolts. Meanwhile, the Spanish crown taxed the settlers according to the number of natives they had working for them. Taxes created a resentment among the local Spanish population, who later revolted against the imperial authorities.

COLONIAL EXPLOITATION

Like many other parts of Latin America, Chile was conquered by a few bold Spanish adventurers. They expected their reward to come either as gold or land. So it was that the territory became divided up into huge estates in the hands of these Spaniards or their direct descendants. The mestizos, or mixed race people, were permitted only tiny plots, while the Indians were left with none at all – except those that they defended with their lives.

In this way the pattern of Spanish colonial life – which was to last for almost 250 years – was established through much of Chile, but the country's colonial exploitation differed from that found in many other parts of Latin America. The mineral wealth, which was to be so important for the country in the 19th and 20th centuries, was as yet virtually unexplored; indigenous communities were therefore largely spared the type of work in gold and silver mines that had killed off many of the native populations of the Caribbean islands and of Mexico. Nor was the Chilean climate hot enough for sugar cane or other tropical plantations, so there was little of the trade in black slaves who were forced to work in the plantations in the Caribbean, Colombia, and Brazil. A population estimate of 1620 pronounced that there were about 20,000 blacks and mulattoes in Chile at that time, but these groups seem to have gradually been absorbed; although Chile was the first Latin American country to abolish slavery in 1823, this was far more important symbolically than in practice.

CROSS-MARRIAGE AND A NEW IDENTITY

In Chile, as elsewhere in Latin America, the mixing of races happened all the more quickly because for many years it was something of a wild frontier, where young men came seeking their fortune and did not bring women with them from Spain. By the time of the wars of independence from Spanish rule at the beginning of the nineteenth century, a large majority of the population was of mixed descent.

The growing sense of a national identity rarely extended to the indigenous people who had survived the centuries of domination. With the processes of war, forced labor, disease, and now intermarriage, this population represented only about one-tenth of the original numbers living in Chile before the arrival of the Spaniards. Nearly all of the remaining groups, known generally as the Araucanians, lived south of the Bio-Bio River. Some small ethnic groups even farther south still had an existence virtually untouched by outside influence.

The Araucanians continued to live by hunting and fishing, although under the influence of the Spaniards they also cultivated wheat and other crops. The groups often crossed the Andes and had links with other groups on the vast Argentine plains. Despite the continued efforts of Spanish missionaries, the traditional Mapuche beliefs and ways of life were still strong. The Mapuche still held land in common and refused the kind of hier-

archical ordering of society that was so typical of both Spanish colonial and Chilean republican rule.

PEACE AND THE NEW REPUBLIC

Only in the second half of the nineteenth century did the new independent Chilean republic, with a population of still only around 1.5 million, begin effectively to occupy all its territory. The final peace treaty with the Mapuche came in 1882, when the government in Santiago sent out Colonel Urrutia to subdue the

Mapuche farmland around the Bio-Bio River today – testament to the survival skills of the population.

*Logging – one manifestation of the
exploitation brought by Western civilization.*

last Mapuche forces – if the need arose – and to make a lasting
peace after more than three centuries. Urrutia was at the head of
eight hundred men, scarcely more than the original number of
Spanish conquerors. They still had to spend several weeks forcing their way through virgin forest; there were no roads or even
tracks that would allow passage for their artillery and supplies.

Meanwhile the Mapuche gathered more than three hundred
war chiefs. All the indigenous groups seemed determined to fight
one last great battle. They felt they must defend the territory they
had left: to them, the republican Chileans were equally unwel-
come outsiders – known as huincas – as the Spaniards who had
come in the name of the Spanish crown.

But the battle never took place. At the last moment, the
Mapuche chief Pebcheluf sat down with Colonel Urrutia, and
they discussed their position for several hours. Behind them, both
armies were in full battle order, with many of the Mapuche strain-
ing to fight. The colonel insisted on reestablishing the town of

Villarica, which had been destroyed more than two hundred years earlier, and claimed the whole of the territory to the west of the Andes mountains in the name of the independent Chilean nation. In return, the Mapuche were promised the right to live in peace with their customs and social organization respected. The two men agreed on the plan, and the opposing troops were able to relax. Apparently the Mapuche particularly enjoyed the brass band that the Chilean army had brought along.

In 1912, the Chilean government finally granted titles to land for the Mapuche, the survivors of so many generations who had lived and died in the same territory. But the government also offered land in the south to fresh European immigrants, this time from Germany, Switzerland, and the British Isles. These people brought sheep or began to cut down the forest for lumber and paper-making. They introduced the railways, the telegraph, and eventually paved roads. The sovereignty of the Mapuche over their last remaining lands had come to an end.

The surviving indigenous population of Chile still
feel the pain of degradation suffered by their ancestors.

THE KING OF ARAUCANIA

ONE OF THE most bizarre attempts at colonization in Chile took place in 1860, when a French lawyer and adventurer, one Orllie-Antoine, arrived in the port of Valparaíso. He had decided that the Mapuche and other tribes of the south needed a European king to bring them the benefits of civilization.

The royal seal of Araucania – the kingdom, born out of misunderstanding, was short-lived.

THE SELF-PROCLAIMED KING

He set out on horseback with one companion, Rosales, and a donkey. Soon he found himself among the Mapuche, who greatly took to this Frenchman with his long mane of hair. Although they understood little of what he was saying, they responded enthusiastically to the idea of taking up arms against the Chilean state. Many Mapuche chiefs agreed to his plan. On November 17, 1860, he proclaimed himself King of Araucania – Orllie-Antoine I.

His reign was to last little more than a year. In January 1862, as he set out to try to convince more tribes to join him, Rosales secretly sent a message to the nearest large garrison of Chilean troops, who intercepted the king while traveling unescorted.

TRIAL, FAILURE, AND SUCCESSION

Orllie-Antoine was dispatched north to Santiago and put on trial for disturbing the public order. The verdict was that he was not in full possession of all his faculties. This gave the French authorities the excuse to ship him to France, where he was immediately set free. Back in Paris, he began to scheme his return. He spent years trying to raise money – mainly by issuing titles to imaginary parts of his kingdom, and thus creating a whole monarchic structure: many people were persuaded to part with large sums for what were quite fictitious privileges.

In 1869, he set out to Buenos Aires and the Argentine pampas. He was received with enthusiasm by the tribes of Patagonia and soon added this region to his Araucanian kingdom. In theory he now ruled an area (Patagonia and Araucania) far greater in size than France itself.

Once again however, the Chilean army soon nipped his royal career in the bud. They advanced to meet him, setting up new forts along the way. Rather than fight, Orllie-Antoine I turned tail, abandoned his kingdom, and headed back to Paris, never to return. In vain he spent a great deal of time and effort in trying to persuade others to join him in colonizing the vast new territories of what he called "New France."

On September 17, 1879 he died in the obscurity of a public hospital near Bordeaux. He had, however, the foresight to make his monarchy a hereditary one. He had no direct descendants, but was succeeded by a loyal supporter, one Gustavo Aquiles Laviarde D'Alsena – also known as Aquiles I of Araucania and Patagonia, Prince of the Aucas and Duke of Kialeu. So the line of kings of Araucania passed on down through the next hundred years.

The latest pretender, Prince Philippe, still awaits the call from his subjects to assume his rightful place on the Araucanian throne.

The Frenchman Orllie-Antoine – the self-styled King of Araucania – who managed to become quite a thorn in the side of the Chilean state.

The ancient gods of Chile
are revealed through myths
and legends as creators and
guardians of the land.

MYTHS AND LEGENDS

RELIGIOUS BELIEFS and ancient legends have, in the absence of a written language, been passed down by word of mouth from one generation to the next. The older village men have a special role in maintaining this knowledge, which is reinforced during major celebrations such as the ngillatun nature ritual and the complex marriage ceremonies. So important is it that a community is able to trace itself to its roots in the distant legendary past that history and myth become intertwined in a way that has been lost to Western civilizations. Today there is a renewed enthusiasm for many of these ancient legends, as Chileans look toward their tribal roots, just as Native North Americans are reviving their cultural traditions.

Many Chilean tribes originally had a highly developed religious system. This included a whole host of gods as well as stories about how the world began, and how it will end. Often, too, it featured a detailed moral code, laying down the correct behavior in this world and the next.

Common to virtually all tribes is the idea of a supreme being, who created the world and everything in it. Among the Mapuche, for example, he is known as Ngenenchen. Inevitably, after five centuries of contact with Christianity, many native creation legends resemble adaptations of familiar biblical stories. Others draw on the challenges nature poses – for example, volcanoes and earthquakes frequently appear as powerful gods. And some portray the struggle between good and evil forces that permeates all levels of life.

TRADITIONAL TALES

THESE THREE STORIES are among many that are still very much alive in Chile. They continue to play an important role in defining a separate identity and a sense of pride in a past that outsiders have all too often looked down on or suppressed.

THE CREATION

Francisco Lopez de Gomara, a sixteenth-century Spanish chronicler, recorded how the tribes in northern Chile and Bolivia saw the creation. At the dawn of the world Con, the first son of the sun and the moon, came from the north. He sped over the land and, to shorten his journey, created all the mountains and valleys. Then he created men and women and gave them green fields, rain, animals, and crops.

But then one day mankind made him angry, so he turned the land into dry deserts, leaving only the rivers so that the people could survive if they worked hard. His action annoyed Pachamama, another son of the sun and moon. He defeated Con, turning him out of the land and changing all his followers into black monkeys. Then people began to worship Pachamama, until the Christians made them see the errors of their ways. Many years later, there was a huge rainstorm. The only survivors were those who lived in caves or on mountains. One day, these people decided to send out two dogs to see if the flood

The black monkey, representative of the losers in the Creation legend.

*The Sun and the Moon gods are central to the
beliefs of the indigenous Chilean population.*

had stopped. When the dogs came back covered with mud, the
people knew that the water level had fallen. They descended from
the mountains and began to plant crops. With Pachamama's help,
they drove their enemies – the monkeys and snakes – from their
land to the far side of the mountains, where the evil spirits gather.

De Gomara stated that the only fear the Indians have is for the
end of the world. The land will once again become desert, and
the sun and moon will disappear. Such fear explains their
desperation whenever there is an eclipse of their two gods, the
sun and the moon.

51

THE WHITE HORSE AND THE BLACK DOG

When Ngenenchen created the world of all, he last of all made dogs and horses, and finally man. Ngenenchen kept only one thing from man: the secrets of when he would die and where his soul would go beyond death. But Ngenenchen did tell these secrets to the animals closest to man: to the dogs and the horses.

A Mapuche chieftain named Leuque-Leuque had led a long and honorable life. But as he grew very old, he became increasingly worried. When would the day of his death arrive? Were his ancestors waiting for him? What was the world of dead souls they lived in like? One night he mounted his favorite white horse, Kawell, and took his most cherished black dog, Trewa, with him. He called out, "Trewa, Trewa, why are you so sad and nervous at night? Is it true the spirits of the dead come and visit you?" Trewa's ears pricked up, but he did not reply. "Trewa, will I live until springtime?" The dog barked loudly in fear. Angry by now, the chieftain spoke directly to Kawell. "I am your master," he said, "and you must do as I command. I want to know if you can see what the future holds."

The horse spoke to Leuque-Leuque. "It is true that Ngenenchen revealed these secrets to us but kept them from you. He knew that if men could see the future,

Ngenenchen created the world, from the araucaria trees to the tiny strawberries.

they would be terrified at what they saw. The world after death where the spirits live is dark and sad. It is full of the smoke of green wood, and huge black birds swoop to carry off those they catch unawares. Dead warriors live in another part of this world, in the clouds above us, where they are condemned to fight a battle that will never end. The noise of that battle is what you hear as thunder." Leuque-Leuque turned white. He patted the horse's neck and asked him, "Please, tell me how long I have left in this world." Kawell replied, "Wipe your eyes with my tears of sadness. That will reveal the great secret; you will see the past, present, and future pass before your eyes."

Without pausing for thought, Leuque-Leuque rubbed his eyes with the salt water from the horse's face. When he opened his eyes again, the first thing he saw were his dead loved ones, his relatives and friends. As they approached, he was paralyzed with horror when he saw they were phantoms without voices or feelings.

From then on, he could not rid himself of these visions. Wherever he went, he saw suffering souls. Gradually, he refused to go out of his hut, and one day he stopped eating too. One stormy winter's day he died.

Following the usual customs, Leuque-Leuque was to be buried with his favorite horse and dog. But his last request was that Kawell and Trewa should be spared. The storm continued throughout the four days of his burial. Kawell the white horse tried to keep dry under the cover of the araucaria trees. One night, a bright green thunderbolt split the clouds and instantly killed the horse that had revealed Ngenenchen's secret.

Ever since, the most nervous of all animals have been white horses. They snort and sweat whenever they sense a storm coming. In the bright moonlight, they whinny and stamp their feet because they can see Leuque-Leuque among the phantoms.

The havoc than can be wreaked by the volcanoes of Chile has given rise to many legends including that of Millaray and Loncopan.

MILLARAY AND LONCOPAN

For days, the volcano had been spitting out ash and fire. The villagers looked on afraid as it swallowed up fields and animals. They were on the point of fleeing, when suddenly the volcano fell silent, and the sun began to shine again.

The cacique Llancafilo called everyone together. "No one has died, but we have lost houses, crops, and animals. We must hold a big ngillatun to make sure that Pillan, the god of the volcano, will not return to trouble us." One elder promised to give a black goat for sacrifice; another said he would provide a young colt for the second day of the ceremony; and Llancafilo announced that for the third and final day he would sacrifice a young bull. They consulted the old machi woman, who lived in a cave on the slopes of the volcano, about the sacrifice.

"I knew you would come," she explained. "Pillan is angry that you have not been making sacrifices to him and have neglected me. The three animals you offer are insufficient to calm his anger. Come back here tomorrow; tonight I will speak with his spirit."

The machi herself was angry with Llancafilo for not respecting her. She saw a way to have her revenge on him. The next day she spoke to the elders in a distant voice, possessed by the spirits. "The voice of the volcano Pillan will only fall quiet if you, Llancafilo, sacrifice your eldest daughter, Millaray. She must be the third and final sacrifice of the ngillatun."

Llancafilo was heartbroken. But he and the other men of the village knew they must obey. He called in Millaray, who came with Loncopan, to whom she was betrothed. Loncopan suggested they that run away to hide in the far side of the mountains. But Millaray insisted she would accept her fate. The next day, the villages climbed the slopes of the volcano to hold the ngillatun. Pillan was still throwing out rocks and lava. On the first day the villagers danced and sang, and killed the black colt in his honor. On the second day, they sacrificed the young bull. On the third day, it was Millaray who faced her death.

The machi gave her a potion made from herbs to take away all sense of pain. Then she laid the young girl down on a bier, dressed in her finest robe and wearing all her jewelry. Loncopan gave her a last kiss and whispered in her ear, "We will be together tonight in the crater of the volcano." Then the machi raised her knife and with one blow killed the girl. She took the heart from her breast and placed it on the fire to be consumed by the flames.

Llancafilo and his family spent the whole day watching over her body by the graveside. As the sun went down, they buried her, with food and drink for her journey. No one noticed that Loncopan had disappeared. That afternoon, he had climbed to the summit of the volcano, and by the last rays of the sun, threw himself into the crater.

On moonlight nights, the twin shapes of Millaray and Loncopan can still be seen dancing in the smoke at the top of the volcano.

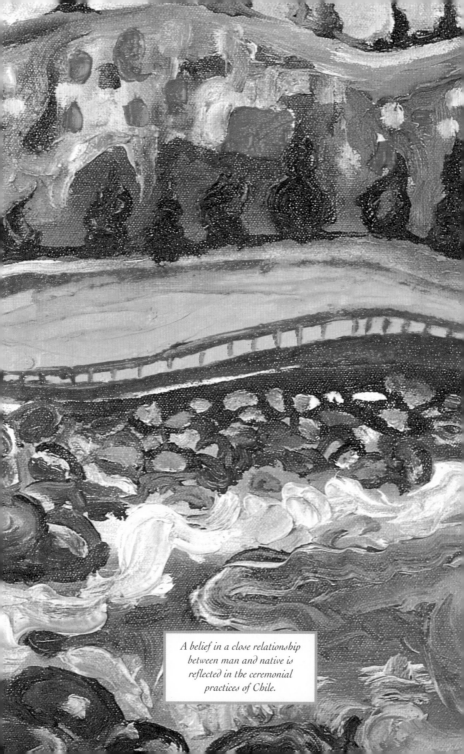

A belief in a close relationship between man and native is reflected in the ceremonial practices of Chile.

BELIEFS
AND CEREMONIES

NATURE PERVADES Chilean tribal culture. People evolved from the world, so its animal, vegetable, and mineral elements are paramount. Folk medicine draws upon the plant world, and nature is the central theme of many ceremonies. Shamans, known by the Mapuche as machi, claim the power of combating evil spirits. Tasks that are entrusted to them include healing the sick and protecting a newborn child from such forces. The Mapuche believe that ancestral spirits must be constantly appeased: otherwise these will return to the land of the living.

Despite the emergence of the modern Chilean state and the inevitable trends toward Westernization, much of the country retains its ethnic soul. Traditionally crafted clothes are worn at all-important ceremonies, including those marking births, weddings, and deaths. In the ngillatun, where a community gives thanks to nature or seeks to appease the spirits, the ritual includes dancing, prayers, horsemanship, music, and sacrifice.

The animal kingdom plays a major role in tribal life. Beasts are used for ceremonial sacrifices; at a funeral it was usual to sacrifice the deceased person's favorite dog and horse. When the Spanish invaders brought over the first horses to Chile, such animals were regarded with awe by the natives. Still today the horse is highly revered.

Community ties are strong in work as well as in play. Sports reinforce the group spirit, and tasks are shared in a system based on notions of duty and obligation rather than financial reward.

BIRTH, MARRIAGE, AND DEATH

S YMBOLIC rituals accompany the passage of Araucanians from one state to another – through the all-important events of birth, marriage, and death. These elaborate ceremonies reinforce the shared beliefs of the community and serve to make the central figures aware that they are part of a caring group that goes well beyond the immediate family.

BIRTH AND THE GODFATHER

When a child is to be born, any married sisters are expected to help. A machi, or shaman, is often also brought in to ensure that the newborn child is protected from the outset against all the evil forces that are trying to steal away its spirit.

After the birth, one of the most important tasks is to choose a godfather, a responsibility taken extremely seriously by all the parties and which strengthens bonds within the community. The father chooses someone who is well respected and whom he can trust; together with his close relatives, he visits the godfather-to-be. After an inquiry into the health of the godfather's community the father declares that he has come to ask him if he will consent to take on the role, in which the godfather will be responsible for educating the child.

The ceremony itself will then be held at the next new moon. The mother dresses in all her finery, putting on her silver necklaces and elaborate headdress. She takes the young baby and undresses it. She sips a mouthful of fresh water from a bowl, warms it for a few seconds in her mouth, then gently sprays it all over the baby's body. By this action, she cleanses it of all harm. Then she wraps her baby in a special woolen shawl that she or her sister has woven for this important occasion.

The traditonal ceremonies of birth, marriage, and death serve to draw the community together and reinforce the link with their ancestral lands.

Mother and child then join the husband, also dressed in his best clothes, who carries them on his horse, decked out in silver trappings, to the godfather's house. There they dismount and the father presents the baby wrapped in its shawl to the godfather, with the words "take this your namesake." From the very moment and by the action of taking the baby into his arms, the godfather accepts responsibility for the child. Inside the godfather's hut, the child is presented to the godfather's family. They all receive it into their group with great solemnity: from this moment on, the child is part of their family too.

Next, the feasting begins. As with many of the native ceremonies, this begins with the sacrifice of an animal, usually a goat.
The animal's throat is slit, and the father and godfather drink the
warm blood as a pledge of their new ties. Then the meat is roasted, the chicha is brought in, and the festivities commence.

MARRIAGE

Because it forges an alliance with a group of people not directly
linked by blood, marriage is important not just for the couple.
Outsiders are regarded with great suspicion because of worries
about sorcery and evil-doing, so negotiations leading up to a wedding are often complicated and lengthy. The
extended family of the bride considers that it is doing a favor to
those asking for her in marriage, and requires compensation.

Once this compensation has been agreed on, the wedding ceremony must be followed to the last detail. First the groom appears
on horseback with two or more of his close companions. They
bring with them sheep, or oxen for the bride's father.

The animals are killed, and the choicest bits offered to the
most important members of the bride's family. Once this first gift
has been tasted and accepted, the food is shared out among the
other guests.

The groom's companions ride off again. They take more offerings to the bride's oldest married sister. By accepting them, she
gives the marriage its "seal of approval" in the wider community.

The groom's parents come to the wife's family's home. They
bring a symbolic payment to the bride's mother, who takes it and
invites them to join the feast. When the wedding party has eaten
and drunk to its fill, the bride is carried off on horseback by the
groom to begin her life as a married woman. Four days later, however, the newlyweds and the groom's parents return to the bride's

parents' home. They bring more offerings, and everyone sits down to another ritual meal. Only when this is over is the wedding considered successfully sealed.

This ceremonial return to the bride's home is a legacy of the days when a groom often simply seized his bride-to-be from her father's home and carried her off. On the fourth day he would come back to eat with his parents-in-law and settle on a price for his bride. Padre Rosales, a Spanish priest from the nineteenth century, described the celebrations that followed:

"When the formalities are finished, they sit down to eat and drink, and toasts are given and they rise and dance to the sound of their drums, flutes, and other instruments. And thus they continue day and night until the chicha is finished, and if there is enough drink to last them for four or six days they do not break up until they see the bottom of the jars."

These traditions have survived the advent of the Chilean state and the introduction of the registration of marriages. The marriage ritual ensures that the union is supported by a strong social framework which is in turn strengthened by the marriage. Individual socially unaccountable choice, the lodestar of Western society, is secondary to the good of the tribe. Less common nowadays is polygamy. In earlier centuries, the local chiefs would take up to 20 wives as a sign of status, and women were treated as possessions rather than equal partners.

Dancing to the sound of flutes and drums is one part of the marriage ceremony.

DEATH AND THE SPIRIT WORLD

An equally complicated ritual is observed whenever a Mapuche or Aymara dies. Because death through any cause but extreme old age is considered an act by evil spirits, the corpse is at first regarded with great suspicion. A machi, or shaman, is brought in to wash the body and to make sure that the spirit of the deceased is not further attacked.

The corpse is then dressed and will lie in the house for four to eight days. When it was difficult to dig frozen ground or to communicate with distant relatives, the body's viscera was removed and the corpse smoked to preserve it until the following spring, when it could be buried,

During the four days and four nights of the wake over the dead body, the mourners make a great show of grief, alternately praising the deceased and all that he or she stood for, then cursing the "murdering" evil spirits and vowing to overcome their power. Peace in the afterlife depends as much on this crucial period immediately after death as on the conduct of the deceased during his or her lifetime: relatives are expected to come from even the most distant reservations and join in the ceremony.

On the fourth morning, the body is placed on a bier outside the house. A guard of honor is drawn up on horseback, and the

The native traditions of rites of passage from life to death are still observed among the indigenous population drawing on a rich heritage of ceremonial practices.

62

community elders give lengthy speeches in praise of the achieve-
ments of the deceased. The body is taken by ox-cart to the
cemetery, where the coffin is placed in its grave, together with some
of the dead person's most cherished objects, and food for the journey that the spirit must undertake. In the past a dead man would
normally have been accompanied by his favorite horse and dog.

After the burial, ashes are usually scattered between the cemetery
and the house of the deceased, to discourage the spirit from returning there. Even so, many
tribes believe that the spirit
only gradually accepts its
new status, and may return
to visit the living.

Accordingly, on the
Day of the Dead at the
end of October the family
prepares a special meal,
setting a place for the
dead person and leaving
the door open by which

> *Song of*
> **CHIEF KORUINKA**
> *The whole earth is a single soul,
> and we are part of it.
> Our souls cannot die.
> All they can do is change,
> but never die out.
> We are all one soul,
> just as there is only one world.*

he or she may enter. Food is served for the deceased, together
with an alcoholic drink and a cigarette. The relatives who participate in the meal address the spirit as if it were indeed among
them. If all this is properly done, the spirit will be pleased, and at
the end of three years will not appear any more among the living.

Such rituals recognizing death are now being re-examined in
post-modern societies, where for the last century death has been
seen as an embarrassment rather than a rite of passage.
The revival of Day of the Dead ceremonies in recent times
addresses the gap left in modern souls by the lack of an
acknowledging ritual.

THE NGILLATUN
NATURE RITUAL

I N THE early days of spring each year, the Mapuche communities gather to ask the gods and their ancestors to provide
abundant crops, or they meet in the late fall as an act of
thanksgiving; for such purposes the ngillatun ritual takes place.
Such a rite is held only at full moon: it is then that Kuyenfucha,
the moon goddess, is particularly open to offerings.

PREPARING FOR THE CEREMONY

At the full moon a month before the ceremony, the elders, family
heads, and the machi, or shamans, get together. They meet to
discuss what the ngillatun will be asking for. It may, for example,
be for dry weather, which involves asking the favor of the old man
and woman of the south wind. Or it may be to give thanks to the
ancestral spirits – known as "the hawks of the sun" – who have
ensured that the crops have been plentiful and there is little to
fear from the winter.

At this first meeting, the elders also distribute responsibility
for the tasks to be performed during the two-day ceremony: the
officials who will keep order; the carriers of the blue and white
flags signifying rain and sun. They also decide which kind of altars,
or rewe, are to be used and which animals are to be sacrificed.

The group of Mapuche hosting the ngillatun then invite
friends and relatives from other reservations as their guests.
During the weeks between, the ceremonial clothes are mended:
woolen ponchos for the men and brightly bordered cloaks for the
women. Certain tasks befall the women. They prepare the special
food of bread, corn, and chicha – the heady fermented beer made
from apples, strawberries, or other fruits; and they bring out their
customary jewelry: silver clasps for their cloaks, and the intricate

*Ramadas, or simple huts, are established as centers
for family gatherings throughout the ngillatun.*

silver breast-pieces with silver coins and bird figures that they
wear for all important occasions. Meanwhile men groom and trim
the horses, each beast a sign of a family's prosperity and power.
Many young people who have migrated to the cities and towns
return to their family groups for the great occasion.

A few days before the ceremony, the chosen officials go to
inspect the site. At the center is the main altar – an ancient
wooden ladder, with human faces carved on it. The sacred area
for the ritual is usually a circle around this altar, which should not
be cut or grazed by any animals. Over the next few days, the officials also repair the ramadas, or wooden shelters, which become
temporary houses during the celebration – places in which the
families can congregate over food and drink.

65

THE DAY OF THE NGILLATUN

The officials are the first to arrive: the success of the ceremony depends on their attention to detail, and their skill at following through the ritual as tradition demands. First they lead in the sacrificial animal or animals – either sheep or oxen. Then they make sure that bowls of grain and drink are placed near the main altar, and adorn this with branches of apple, cinnamon, and other woods as stipulated by tradition.

The woolen ponchos and cloaks worn by the men and women make the ngillatun a colorful scene.

Gradually the other participants arrive, decked out in their traditional woven costumes, set up their ramadas, and begin to cook and renew acquaintances with their neighbors.

THE RITUAL BEGINS

All of a sudden there is a silence. At the main altar, set up to face the rising sun, the main priest begins to chant a prayer in the ancient Mapuche language, a prayer to welcome the gods and the spirits of the ancestors. The priest also calls for the sacred area to be cleansed of any lurking evil forces. This is the moment for the Mapuche horsemen to demonstrate their skill. Most of them have painted faces or wear sheepskins to frighten away the spirits.

They gallop four times, circling the main altar and a smaller one set up about a hundred yards to the east of it. Two of them carry banners – one black to symbolize rain, the other white to represent the force of the sun. The rest follow in twos, with one of the officials bringing up the rear. Following his shouted orders, they whoop out a challenge to the spirits, daring them to fight or to leave everyone in peace. After four or eight laps of the field, the proud riders leap from their horses by the smaller altar.

Meanwhile, dancing has begun around the main altar. The dance symbolizes the link between the living and the dead, and calls for the ancestors' help to combat the evil forces. As they begin to dance, men and women pluck sprigs of sacred wood or stalks of barley and wheat from the altar to protect themselves. By now, the big flat drums are sounding, while other musicians are playing on clay whistles or on the trutruka, the long trumpet made of sheep's horn.

The dancers gradually form two lines between the altars, and the leader of the ceremony concludes this part of the ritual with a prayer, while the two lines of people sway on the spot.

THE SACRIFICE OF THE CHOSEN BEAST

The second part of the ceremony begins as the ngillatufe – the male officer in charge of the machi – slits the animal's throat, and it is left to bleed to death. As it slowly sinks to the ground, the priest cuts off its right ear and offers a prayer to the ancestors. Then he cuts out the heart and raises it for all to see.

He says another prayer for the renewal of life, and with those words touches the heart to his lips. The other officials do the same. The chief priest then places the heart in the center of the altar. A bowl of the fresh blood is handed to him, and he ritually sprinkles the altar and the altar fire with it.

The ngillatun offers the opportunity to remember the symbiotic relationship between man and his environment.

The lines of participants start to dance again on the spot, swaying back and forth and chanting in a low voice. The dead beast is quickly skinned, and its skin brought back and laid beside the altar. A black skin, which signifies a prayer for rain, is placed on the left of the altar, or a white one, making a plea for dry weather, to the right. Some of the meat is thrown on the fire, and the smoke that rises to the sky is taken by the ancestors, the "hawks of the sun," who must also be fed.

THE DISTRIBUTION OF THE GRAIN

After a second round of prayers, the priest chants, then scatters grain around the altar; again, some is thrown on the fire to please the gods. Above all, the prayers are addressed to Kapuka, the goddess of fertility and abundance. Two more rounds of prayer follow, during which the same actions are repeated with kernels of maize, or with the sprinkling of chicha or other drinks on the fire and the altar.

Then everyone begins to dance again. They will continue to do so until the officials in charge decide that the gods and the ancestors have been satisfied with the offerings and the respect shown to them. The family groups return to their ramadas, and the more social side of the ritual starts. The older people are sprinkled with chicha and asked to give their blessing to the food.

The Mapuche community believe that it is the observance of the ngillatun that will bring about a good harvest.

The ngillatun ceremony continues usually for two days. By the end, the close network of the Mapuche community has been reinforced. The young people who have moved away from the reservations have understood the importance of their ancestors, as well as the continuum of life and death. They now hope that nature will go on providing for all the members of the tribe.

*The community ethic of sharing work is still strong among
the native populations of Chile, here seen harvesting peppers.*

SHARING WORK

FOR MOST of their history native Chileans rejected the idea
of individual ownership of land. Their religious outlook
found ridiculous the notion that anyone could claim to own part
of the earth, the provider of life for everyone.

Only in recent times has their system of collective ownership
broken down, partly because of government opposition but
also because the natives have come to realize that they need legal
proof of ownership to defend their territory from outside
exploiters and settlers. This means that each family has to
claim its share, and the original landholding is divided into
smaller plots.

HELPING HANDS: THE MINGACO

But the old collective tradition still thrives, most notably in the mingaco, or shared agricultural work. Whenever there is a task that would be hard for a single family to complete on its own – planting the maize crop, harvesting, clearing more land, or perhaps building a new adobe house – the head of the family invites relatives and friends to help.

Everyone joins in without expecting payment, although they are usually rewarded with food and drink, which helps turn the hard-working occasion into a celebration. Often whole families, including their children, are taken along and the occasion becomes one huge picnic.

Chileans consider it a duty to participate in the mingaco if asked. It is another way in which the community is brought together, and the network of reciprocal obligations is strengthened: once someone has helped a neighbor, that person can then be counted on to come and return the favor.

A LIFELONG PACT: THE VUELTA MANO

A more individual form of this reciprocal work is the vuelta mano. This is an agreement between two men, often part of the same extended family, that they will help each other in work whenever the need arises. The pact is often sealed by the two men drinking chicha or eating food from the same bowl, after which they are said to be misha, or joined together as brothers in their work.

This solemn agreement is often renewed each spring as new tasks emerge and can last until the death of one of the parties. Like the mingaco, the vuelta mano is an arrangment that strengthens relations within a community that relies on mutual support to survive in an often harsh natural environment and feels constantly threatened by the outside world.

SHAMANS
AND SORCERERS

A CONSTANT STRUGGLE between good and evil: that is how indigenous Chileans look upon life. The Mapuche have a pantheon of gods who work for the good of the people. Chief among them are Ngenemapun, the lord of the earth, and Ngenenchen, the lord and creator of the world and of all its life. These gods are both male and female, as well as being both young and old, so they give rise to four characters – the Old Man, the Old Woman, the Youth, and the Young Girl.

These forces for good are identified with the east – where the sun rises beyond the Andes mountains – with the Morning Star, and with the white and blue of the morning sky. They are supported by the spirits of those ancestors who have been given the proper sendoff into the other world and have been treated with due respect since their death. These are known as the pillan, or "hawks of the sun."

The world of evil, of dark negative forces, is under the ground. It is associated with the north – where all the Mapuche's invaders have come from – and with the west, the place where the sun is defeated every evening.

These evil forces, known as wekuufu, appear in the shape of animals or birds, especially at night. Most powerful among them is the wiltranalwe, the robber of souls, who takes on the shape of a tall skeleton of a man, riding the fields and mountains at night in a long, black cape.

Good and evil wage their fiercest battle when one of the Mapuche falls ill. In such an event the fight for health will accordingly become a conflict between these forces – between the shamans, known as machi, and the representatives of the dark forces, the kalku or sorcerers.

72

*It is among the ranks of Mapuche
women that machi, or shamans, are drawn.*

THE WOMEN HEALERS

Nowadays, the machi are almost always women, yet in the past, the special powers necessary to be a healer and a fighter of evil were more often vested with males. John M. Cooper, in his handbook *South American Indians* (1946) claims: "In earlier times, the male shamans were very commonly transvestites, dressing as women and practicing sodomy. By the second half of the eighteenth century, the machis were ordinarily women. In more recent times, the profession has been followed almost exclusively by women." Even if this claim is exaggerated, it does show that among the Mapuche and the other indigenous groups in Chile, those who were in some way different were recognized as having special powers, which could be used for either good or evil.

A woman who has recovered from a life-threatening illness is considered as having the power to become a machi. Her recovery is seen as proof that she has the strength to fight and defeat the forces trying to carry away her soul. If she has been strong enough to defeat evil in her own body, she is likely to be able to overcome it when it threatens to take over others.

THE MACHI WHO
WAS INSPIRED BY A VISION

IN HIS INVALUABLE book on Mapuche society, *Hawks of the Sun*, Louis Faron tells of how a young woman he knew came to become a full-fledged machi.

She came from a poor family and was a sickly child covered with boils. Although a machi, her mother had failed to ward off the evil spirits and to bring about her recovery. But one day the girl was tending the sheep when she saw the vision of a white lamb, who emerged from the bushes, over which appeared a large drum of pure white lamb skin, to which was attached a blue and white drum-stick festooned with bells. She interpreted this as a sign that she had the power to become a machi. Her mother conceded that her own powers were failing.

During her next bout of sickness, the girl decided to seek a cure and training from an eminent machi in Maquegua, near her natal reservation. Her father could not afford to pay, but his brothers and sisters contributed to the cost. She stayed with the machi for about five years, by which time she was nearly as skilled as her teacher; although she lacked some of the elder's knowledge, she knew her own powers to be superior.

As a full-fledged machi, she now earned a good living. She rebuffed criticisms that machis make easy money: during her work she found herself possessed by a spirit and close to death – but as she grew older she became wary of the dangers of spirits entering her.

COMBATING THE POWERS OF DARKNESS

A new machi is initiated over a period of several months, during which her teacher reveals medicinal secrets and instructs her about the powers of good and evil. After her initiation she can be called on by anyone in the community whenever there is a life-threatening illness. Outside her house she hangs the blue and white flags to ward off evil forces. She also sets up the rewe, or ceremonial ladder. This is a wooden structure with several vertical steps, up which the machi climbs during important ceremonies, which symbolizes her contact with the world of the gods. She also has her sacred drum (or kultrun), bells, and rattles to scare away the evil spirits.

A face mask – part of the rich Mapuche tradition of ceremonial artifacts.

The Mapuche still consider illness itself an attack by evil forces on a person, not for anything wrong that he or she has done, but because evil spirits are always on the lookout for the opportunity to steal souls. The machi has many weapons against these evil spirits.

She can prescribe herbal medicines if the threat is not a serious one. She can massage the parts of the sufferer's body where the evil is thought to have penetrated, or suck the spots to get rid of the evil poison. Alternatively, she may spray the body with water or urine, or blow tobacco smoke over the patient in the direction of the four points of the compass.

In the gravest cases though, the machi is likely to go into a trance in front of the patient. This is an exhausting process, and one that no real machi will embark on lightly. The machi

turns slowly around by the side of the patient, chanting long incantations in ancient Mapuche that she has learned from her teacher. Gradually she induces a hypnotic state in herself and becomes possessed by the evil spirits also inhabiting the sick person. In her internal struggle with these spirits, she can divine how best to conquer them. She will utter a description of her fight, and instructions to her assistant as to how to combat the evil. Eventually she falls exhausted to the floor.

When she recovers, the assistant needs to relay faithfully all that happened during the trance, and between the two of them they decide what the patient should do.

A TRIUMPH OF EVIL

The Mapuche and other indigenous groups still place more faith in this medicine than in the Western varieties offered by the

The symbolism of the forces of good and evil – the earth and the sky – demonstrate a firm respect for the power of man's surroundings.

Chilean state. But the machi are not infallible. Louis Faron wrote about a machi who was called out to tend to a sick girl. The machi arrived with her special drum and bells. She prayed to her ancestors, who also used to be machi, to ask them to identify the cause of the illness, to tell her whether it would be possible to cure it, and to vest in her the power to conquer the evil spirits. The ancestral spirits entered her body and she began to wail and shake her arms and hands uncontrollably. Suddenly she accidentally dropped her drum into the fire and her male assistant had to rescue it. Her speech became a series of virtually incomprehensible gasps and strange words. Then she opened her eyes, lit her pipe and blew smoke over her hands and arms, and then over the patient's naked body.

Her assistant gave her an account of what she had said while possessed – that an evil spirit who dwelled in the mountains had stolen the girl's soul. He told her

A shamanic figure from Peru. Shamanism is an established part of Andean culture.

which herbs she should use, and that prior to mixing the remedy with cold water she should place the blade of her knife upon her arms and legs. This she did, and her trembling ceased.

She rubbed the potion over the girl's body, then began to beat her drum and sing. For a few minutes she was again possessed and her assistant had to save her from falling into the fire. He warned her that the patient would die, and the machi conceded to the girl's father that she could not recover his daughter's soul from the evil spirit in the mountains and that the only hope was for him to call upon his own ancestors and the supreme being, Ngenenchen. After sitting in near silence for a long time, she and her assistant departed. Two days later the girl patient died.

Such a death is always interpreted as a victory of the evil forces. There is no such thing in the Mapuche world as a "natural death." It would often be seen as the work of a sorcerer, or kalku: an old and ugly woman who lives alone in the woods or in caves, where she meets with her sisters to plot their attacks.

In earlier times, there are reports that anyone suspected

of practicing these dark arts would be burned. Nowadays, those accused of being sorcerers are cast out of the reservations or left to live as far away as possible from the rest of the group.

While machi are revered in the community, those who practice sorcery are shunned.

INITIATION SONG OF A MACHI

Singing, singing you chose me,

machi from the east.
You sang to the south and so chose me,
machi of the east.
To choose me, four gods called on me.
To choose me, they called my name.
I will plant my sacred flowers,
my cinnamon tree, my laurel bush.
My ancestors will help me;
help me as well, King of the Heavens.
Give me my healing flower, my painted stone.
Here is my sheep, my lance at the ready,
my assistants.
My warriors from the south are all lined up.
So great is the power of my soldiers
they make the earth tremble.
My soldiers charge down from
the sky with the swords of the south.
Everyone is happy at the sight
of my potions as I shake my medicine stick,
my sacred leaves.

TRADITIONAL MEDICINE

To native Chileans medicine is just one part of a whole system of beliefs, not a distinct science in itself. Rather than being the consequence of a mechanical failure of the body's parts, illness is considered as a lack of harmony between the person and life around him or her. When someone is "out of balance" with himself or herself, there is a gap or imbalance of which the evil spirits – the kalku, as the Mapuche call them – can take advantage.

In this sense it is not "natural" to fall ill. Such misfortune is due either to possession from outside, as a result of a lack of attention on the part of the sufferer, or to moral uncertainty. Death, when not caused by old age or war, is a plot against nature. Formerly people believed they lived in such harmony with nature that they could choose the moment of death.

Instead of seeking to treat individual symptoms, traditional medicine attempts to discover what has disturbed the harmony in the first place, so that a solution can be found. This idea of treating the person not the disease is reclaiming lost ground in modern post-industrial societies. Herbalism, homeopathy, accupuncture and other "alternative" therapies are being gradually integrated with the best of western scientific medicine.

THE BODY AS PART
OF THE WORLD'S CREATION

While ethnic Chileans do not believe in the theory of evolution of species, they do see humanity as part of creation – that is, that people bear within their own bodies traces of all the processes that have gone on in this world since its beginnings. Such traces, which the Mapuche know as "ashes of stars," link humanity back not only to animals but also to plants and even to the mineral world from where everything originated.

"Every tree, every plant is a pharmacy" – *traditional medicines have been made in Chilean homes from natural resources for centuries.*

Accordingly if someone falls ill, the curandero, or medical expert, will search for the most appropriate item in the animal, plant, or mineral world to restore the balance. When the illness is cast out into the world around the sufferer, the greatest care must always be taken not to disturb the balance of the rest of nature.

The method of the medical expert therefore differs greatly from that of a Western doctor who examines a patient and then prescribes. In the traditional Chilean approach, the Curandero tries to discover the point at which the sick person's harmony was disturbed, and to identify the evil forces who are attacking and the natural resources that can be drawn on as a cure. The dreams of the curandero may guide the way; for example, a dream of a volcano may indicate that is where the evil spirits dwell.

NATURE'S PHARMACY

The first Spaniards to reach Chile were amazed to see the extent to which the natives used the natural world for medicine. "To them, every tree, every plant is a pharmacy," one of the early missionaries exclaimed. The most important plants used for this purpose are the canelo tree and the wild strawberry, which grows in abundance around lakes and on the southern mountains.

Use is made of the fruit, leaves, and roots of the strawberry. The roots are boiled to make an infusion taken to prevent internal bleeding, to cure stomach problems, and to help a woman giving birth. Dried strawberry fruit is eaten to restore health; while fermented strawberries can be the ingredients of chicha, or fruit beer. Evil spirits – particularly the thieving chonchon bird – are believed to be kept at bay by the strong perfume. The Mapuche also wear the leaves to ward off evil and hang them over their front doors to protect their homes.

Herbal medicines are central to Chilean culture, and a rich variety of preparations can be readily purchased from the local market.

An even more important medicinal source is the sacred canelo pine, whose bark and leaves contain great quantities of vitamin C and were used by Spanish and other European sailors to fight scurvy and other diseases suffered during long sea voyages. However, indigenous Chileans see the canelo as a sacred tree and employ it widely. The wood is used to make the special ladders, or rewe, that the shamans, or machi, climb to communicate with the spirit world. It is often found in the doorframes of huts to help ward off evil spirits.

Fragaria chiloensis, *the large-flowered and fruited strawberry first discovered on the coast of Chile.*

A good example of how traditional medicine operates is in the treatment of warts. First the curandero establishes which is the original wart and cuts a cross on it. The sufferer is led to a canelo tree where a similar cross is cut into its bark. The person must then walk away from the tree without looking back: the evil influence now passes from him or her to the tree, which absorbs it and so brings about the cure.

So important is the canelo tree that each machi has her own special secret one, where she can pass the evil influences that cause harm. Her identification with her tree is paramount. Its felling brings about her death; likewise anything that happens to her is immediately reflected in the health of the tree.

Such knowledge of plants and the traditional lore of indigenous medicine is passed down from generation to generation in the initiation rites for new machi. Even today, although ethnic Chileans accept Western-style treatment from doctors, many continue to have faith in the old ways.

*Horsemanship is a matter of pride in Chile and
contests are regularly held to test a rider's prowess.*

PLAYING THE GAME

THE HORSE, which had been absent from the American
continent since the last Ice Age, made a comeback in the sixteenth century when the Spanish landed. The Mapuche captured
many of the invaders' horses, and although at first the beasts
inspired terror, the natives soon developed a great affinity for
them and became expert riders and breeders.

To the Mapuche, the horse represents far more than a com-
modity: it is an animal with a spirit that is to be treated with
respect, almost like a human being. It may seem paradoxical to
Western minds, but eating horse flesh is regarded as conferring
honor on the horse, because its good qualities are being imbibed
in a highly symbolic gesture. Nowadays, the Mapuche show their
great skill on horseback in ceremonies such as the ngillatun
nature ritual. They also go in for horseraces, not only so that the

riders can demonstrate their prowess, but also as an opportunity to bet. Mapuches are inveterate gamblers, who are likely to bet on just about anything. Combine that with their passion for horses, and these races can often be extremely heated affairs.

HOCKEY, MAPUCHE STYLE

Betting also stokes the Mapuche passion for their other tradition-al sport, the game of chueca. This is like hockey played on grass, and with curved wooden sticks. When a game is to be held, players – between six and eight in a team – will sleep with the sticks at the heads of their beds, hoping for good dreams about the match.

Much of the action is directed toward preventing opponents from getting to the ball, so the game often becomes extremely physical. The possibility of a stalemate is enhanced because of the method of scoring: if one team scores, and then the other scores, the second goal is sub-tracted from the first team's score and not added to the second team's tally. This means it can take quite a time for a team to reach the required winning score of four goals. As with many other Mapuche activities, the game becomes a more general celebration of the community and its togetherness, so that in the end the result hardly seems to matter.

THE CONTEST OF SILENCE

PERHAPS THE strangest of the betting games, *rüm* is hardly a raucous affair. This consists of two people betting on how long they can stay silent in each other's presence. This challenge is taken so seriously that it can last for days until one of those involved forgets, loses patience, or gives in.

HANDICRAFTS
PAST AND PRESENT

Sfaces adorn the rewe, or altars, of the Mapuche. Religious significance is a prevailing theme of many native handicrafts, such as jewelry and wood carvings. Nature invariably provides the raw materials. Function and beauty go hand in hand in craftsmanship, the mastery of which has long been passed down from one generation to the next.

AYMARA WEAVING

The Aymara and their descendants in northern Chile pride themselves for their skill in weaving. The weaver's technique has remained unchanged for thousands of years. Scissors are used to shear the sheep, llamas, or alpacas, whose wool is then spun on

small handheld spindles. Vegetable dyes transform the wool into bright colors of red, purple, or green. It is now woven into centuries-old patterns, many of which, even in their most abstract forms, represent gods or animals that symbolize deities and therefore bring the wearer good luck.

Traditional weaving techniques and materials are still used today.

Many woven garments have a special significance. For example, a young girl must weave her own urku, a woolen dress that she will wear to signify that she has now reached puberty and is of marriageable age. Men often wear special ponchos in different colors and styles for particular ceremonies – such as funerals, meetings to discuss some joint action, or visits to relatives.

The weaving of smaller items such as belts or braids is done by tying one end of the threads around the waist, and the other around a stake fixed firmly in the ground. The woman then leans back to keep the tension on the threads constant, and weaves the colored threads in front of her. Some intricate patterns have long been unique to a particular village. Among the Aymara, only the men use the vertical loom introduced by the Spaniards. Making the traditional ropes and string, still in use throughout the region, is another task performed exclusively by males.

ADORNMENTS IN SILVER

In times past, natives were quick to take the silver coins introduced by the Spaniards in Chile, Bolivia, and Peru and to use them as jewelry – strung on necklaces, or incorporated with semi-precious stones in earrings.

As well as crafting their own highly elaborate style of earrings, the Mapuche in the south made breast-pieces, often bearing stylized bird motifs. Shawls were on some occasions pinned together with special clasps known as tupu, which included spectacularly ornate silver disks.

Because of its value, silver was also used as the material for the staff of office that the local Indian authorities carried. Such an object normally took the form of a long stick with a silver tip and handle. In such instances the skill of the craftsmanship would reflect the importance of the bearer.

Traditional silver jewelry made from "coins" adorn these women's heads, while their breast-pieces represent the "hawks of the sun."

BLACK POTTERY AND SACRIFICIAL BOWLS

The Aymara and other natives were also expert potters. They dug the raw clay from the hillsides on which they lived and fired pots in brick kilns still in evidence in many villages. As elsewhere in Latin America, early ethnic peoples did not have the use of the potter's wheel, but this hindrance seems only to have boosted the dexterity of the potters. The pre-Hispanic tradition of black pottery – that is, clay fired without oxygen – is still found in the village of Quinchamali, near Chillán in southern Chile, and elsewhere there are numerous small villages still dedicated to producing special handicrafts.

As with woven goods, many ceramic creations originally had a ritual significance that has since been lost. A favorite craft with tourists is a ceramic bowl depicting in its center the small figure of an animal. Few purchasers can realize that such an object has its origins as a vessel that was employed in celebrations during an animal sacrifice, to contain the water or chicha that was taken in the mouth and then sprayed over the beast.

WOOD FROM FOREST AND DESERT

Wood has also been used to make domestic and decorative objects. The dry climate of northern Chile is a great preservative, and many humble wooden artefacts have been found at archaeological sites. Today the pinewood from the southern forests is made into boxes, animals, or mobiles for the tourist trade. And the rainsticks, made from bamboo in other parts of South America, are here made from dead cactus wood from the desert.

Nowadays few ancient methods are used to produce objects for use by a community. It is thanks mainly to tourists that these traditional crafts survive at all. The tiny stoves made from the black pottery of Quinchamali are sold widely. Although traditional handicrafts may have lost some of their early, original significance, the worldwide market for them has guaranteed a measure of prosperity for some indigenous groups.

A woman from Quinchamali holds a piece of black pottery, the forerunners of which were made by her ancestors.

The destructivism of Western
culture stands in stark contrast to
the balance and harmony of native
beliefs and practices.

THE FUTURE

A s is the case with indigenous peoples throughout the world, the native peoples of Chile face the new millennium with great uncertainty. The numbers of Aymara in the north have dwindled to a few thousand. The few surviving Alcalufe in Tierra del Fuego may be the last generation in a line that goes back many thousands of years. Although several hundred thousand Mapuche continue to live in the lands they have defended for five hundred years, their communities are weakened by the departure of many young people seeking work in the cities.

These groups have inhabited Chile for more than ten thousand years, but they are still not acknowledged as being an integral part of it. They are being pushed off their lands, and their right to ownership of that land is still questioned by people who came from Europe in far more recent times. These newcomers have imposed a system of ownership and a concept of development that are alien to the original inhabitants, whose right to be different culturally, to hold beliefs that are different from Western ones, is still misunderstood. Their whole way of life is looked down on, although they can see that the way of other peoples brings about the country's destruction, robbing it of the magnificent forests and stripping it of valuable metals such as copper and silver. The accumulated wisdom of the native people, and their ability to live in harmony with their surroundings, counts for little. They are kept on the margins, both socially and politically. At best, they are encouraged to be exactly the same as everyone else.

THE CAMPAIGN
FOR JUSTICE

SINCE THE START of the 1990s, indigenous groups through-out the American continent have been organizing ever more effectively to assert their rights. When the 500th anniversary of Columbus's arrival in America was commemorated in 1992, they made sure that their point of view – that Columbus represented the beginning of centuries of genocide and oppression – was loudly and widely heard.

In 1993 in Bolivia an Aymara became the country's vice-president for the first time. In his inaugural speech to the Bolivian Congress, Victor Hugo Cardenas told his audience: "After 500 years of colonial silence and 168 years of republican exclusion, we have come forward to tell our truth. Ours has been a history of permanent struggle for freedom and justice, for multiethnic and multicultural democracy. Today we are entering the age of a fundamental change."

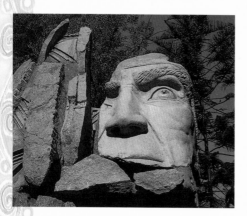

In Santiago, a monument to the native peoples reminds the present population of the sufferings of the past.

Such hopeful words are not always matched by reality. But in Chile new organizations for the indigenous peoples have emerged. Often they owe their strength to the fact that they begin at grassroots level, concentrating on specific problems – educating native children, getting a government credit, setting up a radio station in the local language, or perhaps protesting against unnecessary development.

Their own communal experience has given these organizations practical knowledge of democratic decision-making. They have never accepted the idea of progress at any cost and can therefore suggest solutions that are less damaging to the world. At the same time, the indigenous groups are looking back to their own past. For the first time, the Mapuche and others are writing down their own language. This involves native school teachers learning the spelling and grammar. Legends that older people remember are being collected, and a whole oral tradition is being reinforced. Many women are showing interest in becoming machi. They realize that the knowledge and power of these women is important both for them as individuals and as a way to strengthen their identity as part of a larger community.

The next generation of Mapuche is now learning the traditional values of its forebears.

In this way the past becomes a fertile earth out of which the future can grow. "Listen," says an Aymara mother as she tilts the rainstick for her child on the threshold of sleep. "Listen to the voices you can hear. You can hear the wind blowing across the snowy mountains of the Andes. You can hear the Pacific Ocean crashing onto the shore. You can hear the voices of your grandparents and their grandparents, whispering in your ear about the happy times they knew in our land. Listen: you can hear the sands of the past rushing by, becoming the seeds of the future."

GLOSSARY

ADOBE
A hut built of mud bricks.

ANDES
The great mountain chain that runs the length of South America from north to south.

ARAUCANIANS
The peoples of central and southern Chile, made up of the Mapuche, Picunche, and Huilliche groups.

ATACAMA
A huge desert in northern Chile, one of the world's most arid and inhospitable places.

AYMARA
Indigenous people living in the highland regions of Peru, Bolivia, and Chile, who share a common language and culture.

BEAGLE, HMS.
The ship in which Charles Darwin voyaged in the 1830s, visiting South America and the Galapagos Islands. In the course of his journey he made the observations that planted the seeds for his theory of evolution by natural selection.

CACIQUE
A chief.

CANELO
A pine tree much revered for its medicinal properties.

CAUPOLICAN
A sixteenth-century Mapuche hero who resisted the Spanish invaders but was impaled on a sharpened stake by his enemy as a warning to others.

CHANGO
One of the early peoples of northern Chile.

CHICHA
A fruit beer, often made from apples or strawberries.

CHUECA
The Mapuche version of hockey.

CURANDERO
A medical expert.

FUEGIAN
An inhabitant of Tierra del Fuego.

GUSINDE, MARTIN.
An Austrian anthropologist who recorded his unique experiences living among the tribes of Tierra del Fuego.

INCA
The civilization of Peru and parts of Chile that built a complex empire before the Spanish invasion of the sixteenth century. Cuzco was the Inca capital.

INTI
The sun god from whom Incan emperors were reputedly descended.

KALKU
A sorcerer or evil spirit.

KAPUKA
The goddess of fertility and abundance.

KON-TIKI
The raft created by anthropologist Thor Heyerdahl to test the theory that primitive peoples could have sailed to the Polynesian islands from South America.

KUYENFUCHA
The Mapuche moon goddess.

MACHI
A healer, or shaman, usually female, like a witch doctor.

MAPUCHE
The largest indigenous group in Chile.

MINGACO
A cooperative system whereby members of the group help each other out with tasks.

NGENENCHEN
The lord of men, to the Mapuche: the supreme being and creator.

NGENEMAPUN
The Mapuche lord of the earth.

NGILLATUN
An elaborate thanksgiving ritual, carried out at full moon and involving animal sacrifice.

ORLLIE-ANTOINE
A Frenchman who in 1860 proclaimed himself the King of Araucania and later attempted to establish the territory of New France.

PONCHO
A woven men's cloak with a hole in the middle for the head to go through.

RAMADA
A temporary wooden shelter.

REWE
A ceremonial ladder used as an altar, the focus of dancing and offerings in the ngillatun ritual.

RONGO-RONGO
Wooden tablets found on Easter Island and bearing a script of which the secret is lost.

SANTIAGO
The capital of modern-day Chile.

VUELTA MANO
A pact between two men to help each other with practical tasks.

TIERRA DEL FUEGO ("LAND OF FIRE")
The archipelago off the south tip of mainland Chile.

YAMANA
A tribe of Tierra del Fuego.

FURTHER READING

COLLIER, S., and Slater, William F.: *A History of Chile 1808–1994.* Cambridge University Press, 1995.

COOPER, John M.: *South American Indians.* Published in the *Handbook of South American Indians*, editor J. H. Steward, Smithsonian Institution, 1946.

DAVIES, Lucy and Fini, Mo: *Arts and Crafts of South America.* Thames and Hudson, 1994.

EDWARDS, Agustin: *Peoples of Old.* Benn, 1929.

FARON, Louis C.: *Hawks of the Sun.* University of Pittsburgh Press, 1964.

HEYERDAHL, Thor: *The Kon-Tiki Expedition.* Flamingo, 1996.

MOORHEAD, Alan: *Darwin and the Beagle.* Penguin, 1969.

WEARNE, Phillip: *The Return of the Indian.* Latin America Bureau and Cassells, 1996.

ACKNOWLEDGMENTS

The publishers wish to thank the following for the use of pictures: **AKG**: *p. 10.* **Andes Press Agency**: *pp. 44* John Curtis; *18T, 24, 90* Marcel Reyes-Cortez; *14T, 53, 61, 69, 70, 88, 89, 92* Carlos Reyes-Manzo; *14B, 35* David Ryan. **e.t.archive**: *pp. 33, 77.* **Hutchison Library**: *pp. 66* R. Francis; *43* Eric Lawrie; *93* Edward Parker. **Images Colour Library**: *pp. 32, 37, 76/77.* **Paintings by Rocio Reyes appear on pages**: *15, 22, 36, 41, 45, 51, 54, 56, 59, 68, 78.* **South American Pictures**: *pp. 18, 62, 65, 73, 81; 84* Robert Francis; *34* Sue Mann; *18B, 19, 82, 86* Tony Morrison; *74/75* Chris Sharp.

INDEX